WORKBOOK 5

prepared for the course team by margaret kiloh

This publication forms part of an Open University course DD100 *An Introduction to the Social Sciences: Understanding Social Change*. Details of this and other Open University courses can be obtained from the Course Information and Advice Centre, PO Box 724, The Open University, Milton Keynes MK7 6ZS, United Kingdom: tel. +44 (0)1908 653231, e-mail general-enquiries@open.ac.uk

Alternatively, you may visit the Open University website at http://www.open.ac.uk where you can learn more about the wide range of courses and packs offered at all levels by The Open University.

To purchase a selection of Open University course materials visit the webshop at www.ouw.co.uk, or contact Open University Worldwide, Michael Young Building, Walton Hall, Milton Keynes MK7 6AA, United Kingdom for a brochure. tel. +44 (0)1908 858785; fax +44 (0)1908 858787; e-mail ouwenq@open.ac.uk

The Open University
Walton Hall, Milton Keynes
MK7 6AA

First published 2000. Second edition 2001. Third edition 2004

Edited, designed and typeset by The Open University.

Printed and bound in the United Kingdom by the Alden Group, Oxford

ISBN 0 7492 5367 3

3.1

B/dd100wb5isbn0749253673i3.1v1.3d

Contents

The DD100 course team

John Allen, *Professor of Geography*

Penny Bennett, *Editor*

Pam Berry, *Compositor*

Simon Bromley, *Senior Lecturer in Government*

Lydia Chant, *Course Manager*

Stephen Clift, *Editor*

Allan Cochrane, *Professor of Public Policy*

Lene Connolly, *Print Buying Controller*

Jonathan Davies, *Graphic Designer*

Graham Dawson, *Lecturer in Economics*

Alison Edwards, *Editor*

Ross Fergusson, *Staff Tutor in Social Policy (Region 02)*

Fran Ford, *Senior Course Co-ordination Secretary*

Ian Fribbance, *Staff Tutor in Economics (Region 01)*

David Goldblatt, *Co-Course Team Chair*

Richard Golden, *Production and Presentation Administrator*

Jenny Gove, *Lecturer in Psychology*

Peter Hamilton, *Lecturer in Sociology*

Celia Hart, *Picture Researcher*

David Held, *Professor of Politics and Sociology*

Susan Himmelweit, *Professor of Economics*

Stephen Hinchliffe, *Lecturer in Geography*

Wendy Hollway, *Professor of Psychology*

Gordon Hughes, *Senior Lecturer in Social Policy*

Wendy Humphreys, *Staff Tutor in Government (Region 01)*

Jonathan Hunt, *Co-publishing Advisor*

Christina Janoszka, *Course Manager*

Pat Jess, *Staff Tutor in Geography (Region 12)*

Bob Kelly, *Staff Tutor in Government (Region 06)*

Margaret Kiloh, *Staff Tutor in Social Policy (Region 13)*

Sylvia Lay-Flurrie, *Secretary*

Gail Lewis, *Senior Lecturer in Social Policy*

Siân Lewis, *Graphic Designer*

Liz McFall, *Lecturer in Sociology*

Tony McGrew, *Professor of International Relations, University of Southampton*

Hugh Mackay, *Staff Tutor in Sociology (Region 10)*

Maureen Mackintosh, *Professor of Economics*

Eugene McLaughlin, *Senior Lecturer in Criminology and Social Policy*

Andrew Metcalf, *Senior Producer, BBC*

Gerry Mooney, *Staff Tutor in Social Policy (Region 11)*

Lesley Moore, *Senior Course Co-ordination Secretary*

Ray Munns, *Graphic Artist*

Karim Murji, *Senior Lecturer in Sociology*

Sarah Neal, *Lecturer in Social Policy*

Kathy Pain, *Staff Tutor in Geography (Region 02)*

Clive Pearson, *Tutor Panel*

Ann Phoenix, *Professor of Psychology*

Lynn Poole, *Tutor Panel*

Raia Prokhovnik, *Senior Lecturer in Government*

Norma Sherratt, *Staff Tutor in Sociology (Region 03)*

Roberto Simonetti, *Lecturer in Economics*

Dick Skellington, *Project Officer*

Brenda Smith, *Staff Tutor in Psychology (Region 12)*

Mark Smith, *Senior Lecturer in Government*

Matt Staples, *Course Manager*

Grahame Thompson, *Professor of Political Economy*

Ken Thompson, *Professor of Sociology*

Diane Watson, *Staff Tutor in Sociology (Region 05)*

Stuart Watt, *Lecturer in Psychology*

Andy Whitehead, *Graphic Artist*

Kath Woodward, *Course Team Chair, Senior Lecturer in Sociology*

Chris Wooldridge, *Editor*

External Assessor

Nigel Thrift, *Professor of Geography, University of Oxford*

INTRODUCTION

Welcome to Block 5. You are now almost on the last lap of your course so you are well acquainted with the formula for these workbooks. You know that they are not prescriptive but we hope that by now you have found that they are really useful in helping you to allocate your time, to work through the materials for the block and to practise essential study skills. The explanations and exercises in this workbook are geared to help you with the material on knowledge and the social sciences in Book 5 and with your preparation for TMA 05 at the end of the block.

Block overview

The theme of Block 5, *Knowledge and the Social Sciences*, provides the key to all of your further study in the social sciences, no matter what you decide to do next year. This block provides a thorough understanding of how the social sciences work and how they compare with other areas of study, which will be of enormous value to you in simply looking at life.

In contemporary Western societies people are bombarded with information and advice on all aspects of their daily lives. This knowledge may be confusing. How do people know which food they should or shouldn't eat, which health care might be damaging and which beneficial, how they should bring up their children and conduct their relationships? On the other hand, such access to so extensive and diverse a field of knowledge may be very positive and advantageous. Such knowledge can equip people to challenge the 'experts' and provide a more genuinely democratic society. Knowledge, including skills, techniques and practices as well as access to information and ideas, is what counts in all areas of contemporary life. Block 5 looks at what is involved in this 'knowledge revolution'. The block focuses on the processes involved in the social construction of knowledge. Its main concern is with the ways in which knowledge is made, for example through established and newly formed institutions and sources of orthodoxy, as well as everyday practices and networks. The block explores some of the ways in which knowledge is transmitted, such as the Internet, media, and official and unofficial channels in a variety of written and spoken forms, indicating the centrality of language in the process.

The various components of the block and the recommended route through them are shown in Figures 1 and 2 (overleaf).

Study week	Course material	Suggested study time
26	*Workbook 5* and Book 5: *Knowledge and the Social Sciences:* *Theory, Method, Practice* Introduction Chapter I Audio-cassette 9, Side A and notes	12 hours
27	Workbook and Chapter 2	12 hours
28	Workbook and Chapter 3	12 hours
29	Workbook, Chapter 4 and Afterword Audio-cassette 9, Side B and notes TV 05 and notes	12 hours
30	Workbook and TMA 05	12 hours

FIGURE I   Course materials for Block 5

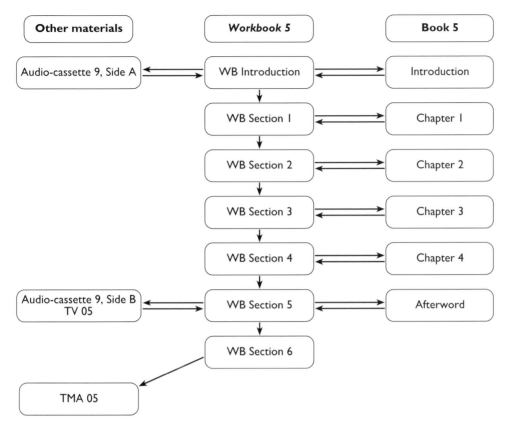

FIGURE 2   Recommended study route for Block 5

It won't have escaped your attention that this block is directly concerned with one of the course themes – *knowledge and knowing*. The course uses the *circuit of knowledge* to examine the processes through which we come to say that we 'know' something. Block 5 focuses on an exploration of the nature of 'knowledge' itself, how there are different kinds of knowledge and how people's beliefs about the way the world is structured are not constant but are constantly changing.

 Now please read the Introduction to Book 5, *Knowledge and the Social Sciences: Theory, Method, Practice*, listen to Audio-cassette 9, Side A, and read the associated notes. Then return to this point in the workbook.

Knowledge and knowing: what do we know?

In Block 5 the investigation into different forms of knowledge is structured by a number of key questions which are outlined in the Introduction to Book 5.

Key questions

1   What is knowledge?

Block 5 is concerned first of all with the nature of knowledge, what different kinds of knowledge there are and what the social sources and significance of these might be. Philosophers, priests, scientists and, finally, social scientists have long been preoccupied by the question, what is knowledge? Frustratingly, each has come up with a very different answer!

When social scientists look at knowledge they try to go beyond the simple dictionary definition and to 'unpack' all of the different ways in which we use this concept. As the Introduction to Book 5 points out, knowledge is more than just 'an organized body of information' as the Oxford English Dictionary suggests. It includes a body of skills, ideas, practices and ways of understanding the world that form part of everyday life as well as bodies of 'expert knowledge'.

If you think about it, there are many different kinds of knowledge. These include religious knowledge, natural scientific knowledge, and social scientific knowledge as well as 'common sense' and 'expert' forms of knowledge, but we expect you can think of others too. We think you would agree that the ones we have listed are clearly quite different things. But to understand the nature of knowledge we need to ask why this is so. What is it that makes them different from one another?

2   How is knowledge socially constructed?

Different societies and different groups of people within them produce different kinds of knowledge and knowledge is not static. For example, medical knowledge in the past was almost completely different to medical knowledge today. Until the gradual acceptance by many people of Darwin's theory of evolution, people within particular religious groups 'knew' that the story of Genesis was literally true and even nowadays different systems of thought lead to very different interpretations and explanations of events.

Each society has institutions and structures that influence the kind of knowledge that is seen as legitimate. These are closely connected with the way that power is distributed in society and the way that this is reflected in language and discourse. Indeed, the ability to control knowledge and ideas is one of the most important weapons at the disposal of those who hold power. Galileo was imprisoned because his contention that the earth revolved around the sun undermined the power of the scientific and religious establishment of the day. In sixteenth-century France, where power was exercised by an absolute monarch and a hereditary aristocracy, the belief system that operated supported the idea of the divine right of kings and the classifications of the feudal system, keeping the majority of the population in misery. Nowadays France is a republic and even monarchists would not subscribe to a belief in divine right.

This is what we mean when we say that all knowledge is socially constructed or *socially produced*.

3　Has there been a decline in trust in expert knowledge?

Some social scientists have argued that a key aspect of society at the beginning of the new millennium is an increase in diversity both within and between different knowledge systems and a consequent increase in uncertainty and decline in trust of experts who purport to convey universal truths. It is certainly true that the increasing complexity of problems has led to a search for new answers, which may challenge natural scientific, political or religious orthodoxy. At the same time there has been a freeing up of knowledge and alternative forms of knowledge are now available to many through the rapid growth of communication technology.

The power of traditional experts, which rested on the monopolization and control of knowledge, has indeed been diminished, but we should not exaggerate either the amount of certainty which existed before or the extent to which belief in expert power has been overturned. Institutions and structures are slow to change and the old expert elites still have considerable power.

Paradoxically, it could be argued, the democratization and spread of knowledge through globalization, the development of the natural sciences and medical advance has not brought about a decline in trust of experts in general so much as a search for new 'gurus' to provide explanations, legitimacy and certainty. There has been a rise in extreme forms of nationalism and fundamentalist religions and a proliferation of alternative therapies and beliefs.

WORKBOOK ACTIVITY I

As a social scientist you need to be able to look at different sides of any question. Practise this by thinking of one example to back up the argument that there *has* been a decrease in trust in expert knowledge and one example to back up the argument that there has not.

For:

Against:

COMMENT _____

There are lots of possible examples that you might use here. An example of the decline in trust (one close to the hearts of those of us who work in a university!) might be the decline in the status and pay of the teaching profession. On the other hand, most patients do still take the word of a hospital consultant, and the newspapers and television seem to be full of experts and pundits to whom much credence is given, so maybe the 'democratization' of knowledge has been exaggerated.

Remember, there is always more than one side to any question and when assessing any form of argument it is important to be aware of the values and purpose which lie behind that argument. Later on we will be looking again at this issue and at ways of *evaluating* different answers and proofs.

4   Can knowledge produce social change?

Knowledge can produce social change in a number of different ways. As we have noted above, challenges to accepted knowledge and received wisdom frequently have a profound effect, resulting in the overthrow of established systems of knowledge and power. This process may be gradual and evolutionary but it may also be the result of the organization and deployment of knowledge and ideas for the specific purpose of bringing about change.

Despite the popular image of scholars in their ivory towers dedicating their lives to the love of knowledge, knowledge is rarely acquired for its own sake. For example, doctors want to understand the human body so that they can cure illness; monks shut themselves up in mediaeval libraries so that they could acquire the key to salvation and when Machiavelli (the Florentine philosopher whose name became an English adjective) wrote his sixteenth-century manual of statecraft, *The Prince*, it was so that he and his prospective master could hold on to the reins of power. Social scientists, by and large, study society not just to understand it but because they want to be able to predict developments. Some study social change so as to be able to influence the direction of that change and to prescribe future action that will lead to a particular result. For them the objective is quite simple – they want to change the world! The work of social scientists is important in informing the policies of governments and commercial concerns.

One of the points which we have been hammering home throughout this course is that social science knowledge (like natural science knowledge) is organized through *theories* – arguments about how things work and how they interact. As you know, there are many competing theories and these are open to debate, testable and changeable in the light of different evidence. As *Workbook 4*, Section 2.4 pointed out, the relationship between theory and ideology is a complex one. Some theories, like those of Karl Marx, may be taken up, developed and organized in the form of *ideologies* (like Marxism) that aim not just to describe and explain the way things are but also to prescribe the way that things *should* be. Alternatively, theories may be heavily influenced and shaped by existing political ideologies. Unlike theories, ideologies tend to be less flexible systems of knowledge and they may have a revolutionary impact on social change.

Knowledge and knowing: how do we know?

As well as exploring different forms of knowledge and changes over time this block also looks at the *theory* of knowledge and knowing (known as *epistemology*) and at the key question of how we 'know' something.

One of the things which the block demonstrates is that different forms of knowledge use different kinds of evidence or proof to substantiate themselves. The philosopher Descartes famously proved his own existence to himself with the conclusion 'I think, therefore I am'. Doctors, religious believers, economists or psychologists look for different kinds of proof.

WORKBOOK ACTIVITY 2

Take a minute to think about the kind of proof that a doctor might consider to be convincing and compare that with the kind of proof that religious believers would accept.

COMMENT

Doctors perform operations or prescribe medicines because they believe that they know the cause of an illness and how to cure it. This knowledge is endorsed by the medical establishment and generally accepted by the population at large. The 'proof' of their knowledge (what we have called 'verification') is the repeated success of their treatments and the recovery of their patients – a painkiller is taken and the pain goes away so this proves that they are right. Religious believers believe that they know that God exists and they also see 'proof' of this in a variety of ways. Some look to the experts of the religious establishment such as priests, some look for literal truth in the holy book, in the authority of a text, some look for evidence of the power of prayer, some believe in miracles and for some life itself is sufficient proof.

What counts as proof in one context is not necessarily acceptable in another. The examples which you will have thought of will all be specific to the here and now. If you had been answering at another time or in another place or culture your examples might have been very different. Early medicine was based on a combination of spells and herbalism and, as Chapter 1 points out, for the ancient Greeks illness and health were ascribed to the balance of different 'humours' in the body. Similarly, in China today there is a whole different system of medicine based on acupuncture and pressure points. These differences are not just variations on the same thing but stem from the fact that all forms of knowledge are part and parcel of the society in which they are situated and they are affected by that society.

Because all forms of knowledge are open to doubt, the social sciences use what we have called the circuit of knowledge as a way of developing and

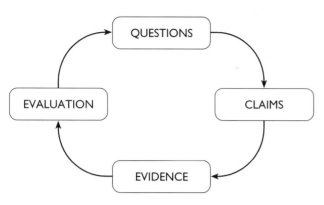

FIGURE 3   The circuit of knowledge

verifying explanations and evidence about society. The blocks so far have dealt with the way in which social scientists:

- begin with questions
- turn them into claims, clear hypotheses, descriptive statements, or explanatory models or theories
- seek out, organize and evaluate evidence
- apply the evidence to the original hypothesis/statement/explanation/ theory
- evaluate the theory confirming, refuting, or modifying it.

The workbooks so far have 'unpacked' for you how social scientists construct arguments (Block 1), use evidence (Block 2), develop theories (Block 3), and how social scientists evaluate theories and evidence (Block 4). The final step in this process, which we will be dealing with in this workbook, is the synthesis and integration of all the information and evidence (including 'failed' theories) and the generation of a new set of questions, claims and theories.

Key skills

We expect that by the end of this block you will have built on the skill of assessing and comparing evidence and theories with which you became familiar in *Workbook 4* and will have had further practice in evaluating arguments and explanations. You will also have been shown how to synthesize information and theories and integrate them into a coherent whole. Put like that it sounds terribly difficult, so let's explore what we mean.

You might wonder why we are talking about synthesis and integration as separate skills. The dictionary definitions of the two words are virtually identical and in everyday language they are often used interchangeably. There are, however, two separate processes involved here:

- *bringing together* different theories, concepts and evidence (synthesizing), and
- *combining* them into something new (integrating).

Think of it like making a cake – you bring together the various ingredients and transform them to make something which is the sum of those ingredients but also something completely different.

Man in Apron
by Larry

Making a cake

In the same way that you can learn to make a cake you can learn how to use synthesis and integrate information and theories. Don't worry if you don't turn into Delia Smith overnight! We will be illustrating how to go about it with activities and questions to help you as we go through the chapters and we are confident that as you near Block 6 you really will have acquired a tremendous amount of new skills:

- You will be adopting a much more critical approach to arguments and be able to assess them.

- You will be pulling together material from different parts of the course.

- You will have stopped accepting what the authors of the chapters say (if you ever did!) and we will have achieved our objective of turning you into if not a fully-fledged social scientist at least one ready to leave the nest and learn to fly.

Assessing Block 5

The best way of learning to fly is by practising and this is what TMA 05 has been designed to encourage you to do. The assignment for this block consists of a 1,500 word essay which will require you to draw on more than one of the chapters in Book 5. This is designed to test both your knowledge and understanding of the course material and your skill in bringing together and integrating different theories and evidence. The workbook is structured so as to help you first to break down and evaluate the arguments which are presented into their component parts and then to practise the skill of drawing on these to put together your own argument. Towards the end of the workbook you will be asked to work through a similar question step by step in preparation for the TMA itself.

Reflective learning

Throughout this course you have been encouraged to reflect on your own learning, including the feedback on your TMAs. Reflective learning means thinking about what you have done so far, identifying your own strengths and weaknesses, and taking any lessons that you have learned to help you with what is to come.

After Block 5 you will be working with the *End of Course Review* and your final TMA which draws on the whole of the course, so the end of this block would be a good time to look back, to identify any gaps in your study which you may have been forced to make and to discuss with your tutor how you are going to tackle the review block.

1 SCIENCE AND SOCIETY: KNOWLEDGE IN MEDICINE

As we noted in the *Introductory Workbook*, all forms of knowledge, be they common sense, the natural sciences or the social sciences, are open to doubt. Any sense of certainty rested on the idea that there were certain truths about the world and that 'experts' could be relied upon to interpret these accurately and to provide reliable information. But was this ever really true? Or is it simply that some forms of knowledge, both in the past and now, are privileged over others by virtue of the power and authority of these expert agents? How is knowledge structured by society?

Chapter 1 uses the narrative of the development of medical knowledge and the medical profession to argue that knowledge and knowing are the product of particular *social institutions*, not rooted in the 'natural' world. Looked at in terms of structure and agency, there is a tension between individual agency and structure in knowledge. Experts are not free agents. They derive their legitimacy from knowledge-structures already embedded in society and as society changes knowledge and knowing change with it. Nevertheless, new ideas have an important role to play in bringing about social change.

Chapter 1, 'Science and Society: Knowledge in Medicine'.

- To identify the main argument of the chapter and separate this from the illustrations used.

- To understand what the chapter has to say about the social production of knowledge, the role of experts, and the role of language.

- To be able to compare the development of natural scientific and social scientific methods.

- To relate the chapter to the other course themes of *structure and agency* and *uncertainty and diversity*.

Now please read Chapter 1, 'Science and Society: Knowledge in Medicine', by Kath Woodward and Stuart Watt and then return to this point in the workbook.

1.1 The social production of knowledge

At first glance Chapter 1 might seem to be 'about' medicine, but appearances can be deceptive. In reality the chapter uses the example of medicine merely as an illustration of natural scientific knowledge in order to explore the relationship between science and society, 'the social production of knowledge and the diversity of knowledge systems' (p.10).

1.1.1 Identifying the argument

Although this chapter contains a lot of information about medicine this 'story line' is used primarily to illustrate a much broader argument. What we want you to get out of the chapter is <u>not</u> a detailed knowledge of the nature of medical science – so there is no point in taking copious notes on the subject! Our objective is for you to understand the argument of the chapter and to be able to distinguish that from the supporting medical examples. The first step is for you to identify the broad argument which runs through the chapter.

WORKBOOK ACTIVITY 1.1

Drawing on what you have learned about note-taking techniques from previous workbooks, choose a quick way of identifying the main points of the argument in each section of Chapter 1 and jot down no more than six points for each section in your own words. (If you absolutely can't think of any other way to say it put quotation marks round it, and make a note of the page reference.)

COMMENT

Previous workbooks have suggested a number of techniques including looking at the book's Introduction, looking at the chapter's contents list, looking at the chapter introduction and conclusion, and looking at the summaries. A single technique isn't always appropriate. On this occasion the book's Introduction is quite general and the headings and sub-headings in the chapter could reinforce the impression that the argument is mainly about medicine. However, the chapter's introduction, conclusion and summaries are really useful.

Note that the summary at the end of Chapter 1 (p.38), whilst still using the example of medicine, provides the basis of the argument which is about knowledge in general and more specifically scientific knowledge. This is (still using mainly the original wording of the chapter):

- There are whole ranges of different systems of knowledge.

- Knowledge is produced in particular circumstances at particular times; it is historically specific.

- Scientific knowledge is characterized by specialized language which defines and delimits what is included and what is excluded.

- New ideas and language are created in response to what has gone before; existing discourses are challenged by new systems of knowledge.

- There are different, both competing and complementary, sets of knowledge which we draw on to define and explain phenomena.

- There are challenges to traditional authority and expertise and the proliferation of different ideas which can create uncertainty as well as diversity.

The Chapter 1 authors have summed this up so neatly, haven't they? But what we want is not *their* understanding but *yours*. If you just copy down what they say, and then later on reproduce it in an assignment, there is no evidence that you have really *understood* the argument. If you translate it into your own words then you will own it – and you will internalize it much more easily.

For example, instead of the penultimate point ('There are different, both competing and complementary, sets of knowledge which we draw on to define and explain phenomena'). We could say 'Whenever we are trying to understand and explain things there is more than one source of knowledge available to us. Some of these sources may contradict each other, others may agree and provide additional information or approaches.' More long-winded perhaps but it spells out what *we* think the authors are saying, rather than simply repeating their original words.

1.1.2 Arguments and examples

One of the key points which is identified above is the argument that knowledge is not 'given' or self-evident but is 'produced' by reference to different kinds of evidence. The next stage in unpicking the argument of the chapter involves separating the development of this argument from the examples which are used to illustrate it. One way of doing this is to build up a grid for each section identifying the main points in the argument on one side and the examples on the other. We have done this below for Section 1.

Argument	Examples/evidence
There are different sources of knowledge	Medical knowledge: (a) subjective, personal experience (e.g. cough) (b) quantitative, scientific evidence (e.g. blood pressure and temperature) (c) expert – professional experience and training (e.g. doctors).
Knowledge is 'socially produced'	Ideas about illness may depend on: (a) popular culture (e.g. relating to stress) (b) common sense (e.g. comments from friends) (c) alternative belief systems (e.g. holistic medicine) (d) 'socially sanctioned' expertise (e.g. GPs).
Expert knowledge has a superior status and authority and is socially sanctioned	Doctors are permitted to prescribe drugs and perform operations. Employers accept a medical certificate as a valid proof of illness.
Expert knowledge has a specialized language and methodology that helps to keep it apart from common sense and to create new knowledge	The working of the body, illness and drugs are described and categorized using a specialized language (e.g. drawing on Latin or Greek). Doctors use observations and instruments to test and assess evidence and diagnose illness.

In filling in the grid we were careful to do two things. Firstly, as far as the argument column was concerned, we separated the general argument of the chapter from any *specific* argument about medicine. Secondly, in the examples/evidence column, we didn't just list all of the detailed examples; we tried to *group* them in a useful way which might help with any later analysis of the argument (e.g. as 'subjective', 'quantitative', 'expert', 'popular culture', 'common sense', 'alternative') and to give just one example for each category.

WORKBOOK ACTIVITY 1.2

Re-read the rest of the chapter then have a go at completing the grid below. Fill in the steps in the argument on the left-hand side of the grid and the examples used on the right. Note that the argument is not always directly stated in a single sentence. You may need to draw it together for yourself.

	Argument	Examples/evidence
Section 2	Diff between common sense knowledge a Scientific knowledge Subjective 'v' objective knowledge	Scientific moves on from many aspects of C.S knowledge Royal Society started to firmly the knowledge – it has reliable evidence backing it
Section 3		

	Argument	Examples/evidence
Section 4		
Section 5		

COMMENT

You should now have a good skeleton summary of the main argument of the chapter and the examples used to illustrate this. You can check this against the filled-in grid at the end of the workbook (pp.69–71) to see if you have misunderstood or missed out something vital. But remember, something in your own words is worth ten of anything supplied by the course team because it is the result of your own direct engagement with the course material.

The main thing to check is that you have successfully sorted the wood from the trees (i.e. the overall argument from the examples):

- Section 2 develops the argument about the relationship between scientific and common-sense knowledge, once again using the example of medicine from which to draw general points. It tells us lots of interesting things about the growth of medical science but this is only to illustrate the main argument about scientific knowledge. The section argues that scientific knowledge assumes that there is a separation between nature and culture, that the natural sciences can claim to be objective rather than subjective, and that it can therefore be used to investigate the world and discover the truth. It is also argued that it is organized in a way that excludes the common people and that the institutionalization and professionalization of knowledge was a prerequisite for the development of the idea of *objectivity* and the 'scientific method'.

- Sections 3 and 4 challenge this idea and develop the narrative of the social production of knowledge by looking at how natural science *actually* works and at the link between politics, science and society. The 'truth' to which the natural and medical sciences lay claim is *produced* by these disciplines and not discovered or revealed in the natural world. In particular, the chapter looks at the influence of gender and the exclusion of women from certain spheres of knowledge and the devaluing of 'female' knowledge as compared to 'male'. The example of medicine is used to show how natural scientific knowledge is transmitted through institutions with authority and power over others and 'common-sense' knowledge is excluded.

- Section 5 concentrates on the relationships between knowledge and *practice* and how knowledge may be used for particular political ends.

1.2 Scientific and social scientific knowledge

As you can see from the summary above, one of the main themes of this chapter is the development of the debate about the character of natural scientific and social scientific knowledge and methods. This in turn relates directly to the issue of how we know and how knowledge is produced. As we noted in the introduction to this workbook, different forms of knowledge depend on different kinds of evidence for support. The social sciences are a specialized form of knowledge and have their own way of gathering information and evidence and constructing explanations. Received wisdom would have it that the difference between science and social science lies in the methods which each uses to investigate phenomena and generate an understanding of how things work.

WORKBOOK ACTIVITY 1.3

Re-read Sections 2 and 3 of the chapter and list the words used to describe *scientific method.*

COMMENT

We had a quick glance and came up with a number of words which are said to characterize natural scientific method – for example, *theory, impartial, objective, controlled, experimental, repetition, double blind, scepticism, falsification, observation, reason, rigorous testing.* There are probably others that we missed.

Some scientists would say that the scientific method is quite different from the methods used by social scientists (and superior to them). But scientific knowledge depends on a process that looks very similar to the circuit of knowledge that we have used to describe social scientific methodology. Both begin by asking questions and developing claims, then look for evidence regarding those claims, then interpret the evidence and use this interpretation to act and change our understanding of the world. If we look at how science actually works the similarities seem even greater.

The main critique which philosophers and social scientists make of science is that it 'assumes that there is a measurable, material world, which can be investigated through scientific methods' (p.19). The chapter argues that Baconian scientific method is *not* objective, culture-free, inductive and rational and introduces a number of alternative views about the process of knowing which apply equally well to scientific and social scientific methods of investigation. These include those of academic commentators such as Foucault, Popper, Kuhn and Evelyn Fox Keller who, although they don't agree with one another, all emphasize in different ways the importance of different *discourses* (culture, language and social interaction) in arriving at versions of what may be perceived to be a truth. Foucault's view is distinctive in that he argues that not only are these particular claims not objective and value-free, objectivity is not possible. What passes for truth is the knowledge which has significant acceptance and support.

Activity 1.4 on SIDS (Sudden Infant Death Syndrome) illustrates the authors' point that there are competing systems of knowledge which are heavily influenced by social factors, including, in this case, the distribution of power and authority and cultural assumptions about gender roles and about expert knowledge. The purpose of the case study is to show how different explanations originate and how it comes about that some carry more weight than others. This example also shows how different social matters have more or less influence at different times. It highlights the fact that the 'true' answer to SIDS may never be found. Fresh evidence is constantly being brought forward, some of which contradicts previous beliefs, and it is most likely that multiple factors are involved rather than only one.

An important conclusion that this throws up is that we need to view the circuit of knowledge rather carefully. There is a temptation to see the circuit as a process separate from the rest of society whereby ideas and explanations are gradually improved and refined as we scientifically evaluate evidence and develop new hypotheses. In fact, it is not separate from society at all but implicated up to the hilt in the institutions and discourses of the day. To make this clear our representation of the circuit needs to be set in the context of its societal framework so that it looks like Figure 4.

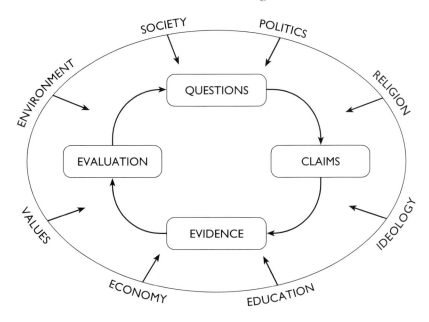

FIGURE 4 The circuit of knowledge in the context of its societal framework

1.3 Linking the course themes

The *knowledge and knowing* theme is closely linked to the other two course themes, *structure and agency* and *uncertainty and diversity*. The structure and agency theme highlights the influence of social institutions and social processes on individuals' and groups' beliefs and actions. In the context of knowledge and knowing this leads us to ask how individual knowledge might be shaped and constrained by institutional factors and just what those factors might be. The uncertainty and diversity theme asks questions about the nature of social change and whether the UK has become a more diverse and uncertain and less stable society in the last 50 years or so. These, too, connect directly with both the knowledge and knowing narrative element, which looks at the changing nature of natural scientific and social scientific knowledge, and the analytical element, which emphasizes the extent to which all forms of knowledge are open to doubt. The medical example used in the chapter provides ample illustration of these points.

WORKBOOK ACTIVITY 1.4

Look back over your notes and previous grids, pick out specific examples that illustrate points relating to *structure and agency* and *uncertainty and diversity* and plot them on the grid below.

	Argument	Examples/evidence
Structure and agency		

	Argument	Examples/evidence
Uncertainty and diversity		

C O M M E N T

You should have been able to fill in your grid by simply reorganizing the notes that you made earlier, but you will need to take a few minutes to digest and think about the issues that are raised.

The example of medical knowledge shows us that there are a variety of different sources of knowledge. We can see that individual beliefs, interpretations and actions are constrained by social structures and cultural discourses. Nevertheless, there is still scope for variation and change in which individual agents can play a part. More importantly, knowledge is shaped by collective agency. Some groups are more able to exercise agency than others.

Uncertainty and diversity have always been a part of knowledge and knowing. Both the natural sciences and the social sciences have attempted to investigate and organize knowledge in a way that makes it manageable and testable but these methods can never be entirely objective. Expert knowledge is a means of legitimizing and restricting access to knowledge as a way of controlling it, but the interaction between social factors and other diverse forms of knowledge provides opportunities for change.

2 KNOWING AND BELIEVING: RELIGIOUS KNOWLEDGE

Whereas the main concern of Chapter 1 was to address the question of 'what is knowledge?', Chapter 2 shifts the emphasis onto the methods that social scientists adopt in order to find things out and to produce knowledge within the social sciences. Using the example of a particular kind of knowledge, that of religious knowledge, Chapter 2 considers some of the ways in which social scientists go about their work of investigating an area of social life, and focuses on methods.

Chapter 1 argues that there are many different forms of knowledge, but it concentrates on scientific knowledge, which, it suggests, might have replaced religious belief as the dominant form in Western society. Chapter 2 explores this argument and takes as its main focus the question of the nature and status of religious belief, how this relates to other forms of knowledge and how it interacts with other social factors. By now you will not be surprised to find that answering this question isn't exactly straightforward and entails asking many more questions before the authors can even approach a conclusion!

Chapter 2, 'Knowing and Believing: Religious Knowledge'.

- To understand some of the different ways in which social scientists go about producing knowledge.
- To be able to compare *positivist* and *interpretative* methods of investigating religion.
- To distinguish between *substantive* and *functional* definitions of religion.
- To use evidence about gender, ethnicity and New Age beliefs to evaluate the theories which are put forward.

Now please read Chapter 2, 'Knowing and Believing: Religious Knowledge', by Ken Thompson and Kath Woodward and then return to this point in the workbook.

2.1 The status of religious knowledge

In the first place the chapter deals with the question of the status of religious belief as a form of knowledge. Then it looks at the practice of religion in the contemporary UK, whether this is in decline or not and how it is influenced by social factors such as gender and ethnicity. Finally it examines diverse forms of belief and the ways in which these relate to conventional religion and to other forms of social change.

2.1.1 Identifying the argument

You can identify the main points in the argument of the chapter by looking at the summaries for Section 2.1 (on the nature of religion), Section 3 (secularization), Section 4 (gender and religion), Section 5 (ethnicity), and Section 6 (New Age beliefs and extrasensory experiences).

The first question which is asked is about the status of religious belief as a form of knowledge and how it differs from natural scientific knowledge.

WORKBOOK ACTIVITY 2.1

Activity 2.2 in Chapter 2 (p.48) asks you to identify *differences* between religion and science. That there is such a difference is clearly illustrated by the extract below.

When you have read the extract:

- Ask yourself why the author of the article does not believe that creationist beliefs are a legitimate form of knowledge.

- Make brief notes on the reasons he gives for his conclusion.

Where Darwin is a dirty word

Keith Devlin

Any British academic who drains their brain across the Atlantic soon finds there is a lot of truth in the quip that Britain and America are 'two countries divided by a common language'. For a British university scientist who makes the big trip, one startling discovery is that a staggering 44% of Americans believe the biblical story of creation is absolutely true. For almost half the US population, both the Big Bang theory and the theory of evolution by natural selection are rejected outright. And this in a country that leads the world in scientific discoveries and technological advances, whose universities and research laboratories are homes to more Nobel prizewinners than anywhere else, and whose vast resources put a man on the Moon.

Fresh off the plane, you are likely to meet some of that 44% the moment you step into a classroom. How do you teach science to someone who refuses to entertain the over-whelming mass of evidence that makes the principles of evolution by natural selection one of the most sure pieces of scientific knowledge we have? It doesn't help to point out that the evidence for evolution is more certain than much of the medical knowledge these students rely on when they fall sick.

I first met this attitude in 1990. Three years earlier, I had left Lancaster University for a two-year research position at Stanford University, and then moved on to a prestigious private college in the US.

As a mathematician, I don't normally teach evolution, but I had to lead a general education course for non-science students in one class. (In the US, many institutions insist all students take some maths and science classes.) I began by showing the class the first part of Stanley Kubrick's classic movie, *2001: A Space Odyssey*, which shows our ape-like ancestors discovering language, learning, knowledge and tool use, and ends with a bone tossed into the air turning into a modern space ship.

I aimed to use the movie to help explain how maths and science are conceptual tools we use in addition to our physical tools. But the class took an unexpected turn when one young man took exception to the film, and to my assumption that Darwin's standard story of human evolution was pretty well accepted. What had been planned as a course on the nature and uses of maths became, of necessity, an attempt on my part to explain the nature of science and how it is done. But it was an uphill battle I never won.

My main antagonist was bright and articulate and – apart from his huge ignorance about the scientific method – extremely well educated and widely read. Frankly, I found it quite scary to encounter such blindness towards evidence in someone with such ability.

I am not talking about belief in God here. But while no scientific evidence suggests there is no God, there is a mountain of evidence that is incompatible with a literal interpretation of the Genesis story of the creation, which implies that the entire world was created in more or less its present form – complete with Adam and Eve – about 10,000 years ago.

The issue of teaching evolution in schools hit the US headlines recently, when the Kansas Board of Education voted to remove all mention of evolution from the state's school science curriculum. In doing so, it joined Alabama, New Mexico and Nebraska, which have also placed severe restrictions on the teaching of evolution in schools.

Over a decade ago, the US Supreme Court decreed that states could not compel the teaching of creationism. Since then, the creationists – a large and powerful, right-wing lobby group – have been trying to push Darwin out, or at least make sure it is presented as 'just one opinion'.

In Alabama, any school textbook that discusses evolution must carry a warning that says 'This textbook discusses evolution, a controversial theory some scientists present as a scientific explanation for the origin of living things, such as plants, animals and humans. No one was present when life first appeared on earth. Therefore, any statement about life's origins should be considered as theory, not fact.'

Because state legislatures cannot exert the same control over universities, lecturers have much greater freedom in what and how we teach it. But we have to teach the students the schools produce. Even at my college, in the highly pro-science state of California, I regularly meet students who think science is 'just one person's opinion'.

This, I think, is where the real problem lies for the educator. How can you teach science to someone who has reached 18 and thinks it's about which ideas you find the most appealing? Having that student in your class four hours a week for one or two semesters is unlikely to overcome the effects of 12 years of school education. University education can build on school; it's hard to overturn what was learned in school. To get the basic ideas of science across, you have to accept the framework in which science operates.

The US academic waters are indeed inviting. But for some students you will meet, you will have to explain what science is and try to convince them that the entire enterprise has merit. Nothing you will have experienced in the UK will have prepared you for that.

Source: *Guardian Higher*, 14 September 1999

C O M M E N T _____

The author rejects creationism not because it is a religious belief but because its adherents will not accept the need for 'scientific' verification – the use of experimental methods and proofs to validate theories and hypotheses. To him this cannot be knowledge and can only be classified as ignorance or superstition.

The extract emphasizes the differences between evolutionary theory and creationist beliefs but it struck us that although there is undoubtedly a difference between the rational nature of science and the spiritual nature of religion there are aspects of the acceptance of both as knowledge which are surprisingly similar (compare the discussion on Audio-cassette 9, Side A). Both are legitimized by a form of authority, both are produced through particular language, both are institutionalized, and there are symbols and rituals in science that can acquire an almost religious significance to some adherents! That these aspects tend to be the *social aspects* of the two different forms of knowledge reinforces the argument of Chapter 1 that 'knowledge' is neither absolute nor divorced from its context but is socially constructed and conditioned.

This point is developed in the discussion of the definition of religion in Section 2. Most people think of religion as involving a belief in God, the existence of some kind of spiritual element in the world over and above what can be discovered by the natural sciences and some kind of moral code that we should live by. Social scientists have been more analytical and Section 2 identifies two main types of definition – substantive and functional.

WORKBOOK ACTIVITY 2.2

To make sure that you understand this distinction re-read Section 2 and then make a note of the two definitions below, using your own words and giving an example of each.

	Definition	Example
Substantive		

	Definition	Example
Functional		

COMMENT

According to Section 2 the substantive definition of religion concerns its content (e.g. beliefs, practices and hierarchies) and the functional definition focuses on its purpose. But how helpful is this? The distinction between the two is exemplified in the work of two of the key thinkers in the social sciences, Max Weber and Emile Durkheim. Each saw religion as having an important influence in different ways but at the same time each included both substantive and functional aspects in their approach.

Weber's approach to religion is said to be largely 'substantive', in that he concentrated on the specific beliefs and practices of Protestantism, but there are also functional aspects. He was interested in Protestant beliefs not for their own sake but, as Chapter 2 says (p.49), because of 'their ethical implications for individuals' economic behaviour, and the role played by this economic behaviour in the development of seventeenth-century capitalism'. In other words, because of the function they performed in a specific society.

Durkheim's definition also included both substantive and functional aspects. He defined religion substantively – the 'sacred' as opposed to the 'profane' – but the main thrust of his argument was functionalist in that it saw religion as serving a social purpose by uniting individuals in a shared community. The logical conclusion of this argument is that almost anything can be a religion, provided it combines the necessary features of 'a unified system of beliefs and practices relative to sacred things, that is to say, things set apart and forbidden' (Durkheim, 1912/1965, p.21).

WORKBOOK ACTIVITY 2.3

Section 2.1 lists some examples of belief systems that perform the same social functions as religion. Can you think of others? Remember the definition above and make a note of the 'sacred' element of the belief as well as rituals, symbols and ceremonies that may bind people together.

COMMENT

We hope you have managed to think of at least one example of your own. If you do that instead of using the ones given to you, you not only get to practise applying the ideas, but you will probably remember them more easily too. The one we thought of was football. The local team is sacred to its supporters; they are united into a close community by their belief; the trainer or manager plays the role of high priest; certain objects and places such as the football ground, the team scarf and strip have symbolic significance; and there are rituals and chants known only to the initiates. This may seem a rather trivial example but for local communities and, indeed, for whole nations, football teams create a sense of belonging and identity and in that sense do serve the kind of integrative social function which Durkheim says is performed by religion.

The definition of religion that is used is important because it will influence any conclusions that are drawn about the 'secularization' of society and the status that religion is given in comparison with competing systems such as natural science. The substantive perspective defines religion in terms of the content of specific beliefs and practices embodying a particular form of knowledge. In contrast, the functionalist perspective sees religion *not* as a form of knowledge but as a social institution, not much different from the family or the education system, with a social role to perform.

In terms of the secularization debate, functionalists and 'substantivists' take a different position. Those who take a functionalist perspective would argue that as long as religion performs a function in society it will persist in some form. Those who take a substantive approach would argue that because there has been a decline in conventional religious practice this means that the status of religion as a recognized form of knowledge is in decline.

2.2 Using the course themes

2.2.1 Belief, uncertainty and diversity

Before the rise of modern science it was through organized religion that people knew and explained phenomena and tried to work out their place in the order of things. This is still the case in some parts of the Christian world and in most parts of the Islamic world, where it is argued that science and religion are not separate and distinct, but are complementary and interconnected. Elsewhere, it has been argued, scientific rationalism has undermined and replaced religious belief as our main way of understanding the world. But is this really true or is it the case, as others have argued, that the failures of science have driven more people to search for spiritual answers to questions about the meaning of life?

As Western society has become more educated, more democratic, and more individualized power has become more distributed. The authority of structures such as the hierarchies of the established churches has been diminished and challenged from both inside and outside. Feminists have attacked the patriarchal nature of the main religions and there has been increasing exposure to different cultures and access to alternative forms of belief. In religion, as in science, there is undoubtedly now more diversity. Religious knowledge and belief have a different meaning in different social and cultural settings and religion may serve different purposes for different groups. In other words, like other forms of knowledge, belief is not static but adaptable according to social factors such as changes in gender roles and increased ethnic diversity.

2.2.2 Structure and agency

Different approaches to religion put a different emphasis on the relative importance of structure and agency. Both the substantive and the functionalist definitions see religion as performing a structural role in society, but the substantive definition places a particular emphasis on the importance of the institutions and hierarchies of organized forms of religion while the functionalist definition would include other kinds of belief systems, such as nationalism or the green movement, which might perform the same social function as traditional religions.

Berger, on the other hand, highlights the importance of individual agency. He sees religion as performing a personal rather than a social function by providing a system of meaning which allows us to make sense of the great mystery of life and death. What is important is not the established structure of the church (or other belief systems) or the role that they play in society but the individual's sense of spirituality and personal identity.

This aspect is present to some extent in most religions and it is particularly stressed in those which have rejected all forms of priestly hierarchy (the Quakers for example). It is also present in forms of New Age belief, many of which emphasize the inner life of the individual and ideas of harmony with nature rather than traditional forms of religious organization and observance.

WORKBOOK ACTIVITY 2.4

What evidence is given in the chapter to support the view that:
- Changing gender roles have affected religion?
- Increased ethnic diversity has influenced religious knowledge and meaning in the UK?
- There was an increase in New Age beliefs in the latter part of the twentieth century in the UK?

How convincing do you find that evidence?

COMMENT _____

These questions aren't as straightforward as they look! There is certainly lots of evidence produced about these issues but first of all you need to keep at the back of your mind the *prior* question of the definition of religion. In this respect you should note that although the evidence on the role of gender covers both Western and Eastern traditional forms of religion and New Age beliefs, the latter is not explicitly covered in the section on ethnicity. Does this matter? Maybe not, but it would have been interesting to see whether there is any connection between increased ethnic diversity and the stated growth in New Age beliefs. We might ask ourselves why it wasn't included. It could be that there is no evidence on this or that the authors simply chose not to include it.

Gender. Evidence is presented to show that although in the past women were poorly represented in the hierarchies of most religions, their increasing involvement in other public spheres has meant that male dominance in the church has also been challenged. The admission of women to the priesthood, for example in the Church of England, has consequently led to changes in practice and in belief. In particular the doctrine that patriarchy is religiously sanctioned by God has been rejected by many believers, leading those who continue to subscribe to this view to transfer their allegiance to other churches. Some women have extended the arena of belief and spirituality beyond the bounds of conventional religion to form broader alternative movements with a spiritual dimension such as eco-feminism.

" D'you think there's anything in this astrology business?"

Ethnicity. As Table 2.4 and 2001 Census data illustrate, UK society is increasingly diverse and there are a large number of different religious communities. Different religions may offer different explanations and world-views and they may perform specific social functions for minority ethnic groups. For example, religious identity may reinforce social solidarity within separate communities or it may provide an alternative value system to that of the majority community.

New Age beliefs. There are many different kinds of New Age belief so once again we need to be careful about what we are talking about. This lack of precision makes collecting evidence more difficult. The chapter talks about New Age beliefs both in terms of the sacred spreading over into the secular sphere, as for example in some forms of ecologism, and in terms of the appropriation of natural scientific ideas into some alternative belief systems. The definition used covers a wide variety of such beliefs. Maybe too wide to be meaningful?

The evidence offered for the view that there was an increase in New Age beliefs at the end of the twentieth century includes the growth in the number of books on the occult and surveys and interviews conducted by the Religious Experience Research Unit at the University of Oxford and the Religious Experience Research Project at Nottingham University. How we evaluate this information and what conclusions we reach about the nature of religion as a form of knowledge and the way in which it interacts with society depends to a large extent on the methodology which is used to analyse the data. This is dealt with in Section 2.1 of the chapter and is discussed below.

2.3 Investigating religion

On the one hand, it is claimed that social change and advances in natural scientific knowledge have run counter to religious beliefs and have led to increased secularization. On the other hand, there seems to have been a growth in interest in alternative beliefs which can be seen as a response to the undermining of conventional forms of religion and scientific knowledge by the increasing diversity and uncertainty of modern society. We can all give our own opinion about the question but in order to assess the various claims which are made we need to investigate the evidence for the arguments which are put forward.

Chapter 2 distinguishes between *positivist* and *interpretative* approaches to the investigation of religion (Section 2.2.1). They sound complicated but don't be alarmed. These are just social science names for something that is quite easy to grasp. To help you we have constructed a grid summarizing the main features of each.

WORKBOOK ACTIVITY 2.5

Check through the grid below and then fill in the strengths and weaknesses of the two methods and an example of each taken from the chapter.

	Positivist	Interpretative
Assumptions	We can only learn about the world and about people and social relations through observation of what people do.	Acknowledges the agency and understanding of human subjects. Takes account of the intentions of both subjects and researchers.
Methods	Observation and measurement. Uses quantitative methods, e.g. collection and analysis of statistical data. Seeks to make causal links, to construct general laws and establish structural explanations.	Uses qualitative methods which allow for a variety of perspectives and meanings, e.g. interview techniques including open-ended questions and unstructured interviews.
Strengths		
Weaknesses		

	Positivist	Interpretative
Example		

C O M M E N T

The kind of method chosen to investigate religion depends very much on the definition of religion which is used by the researcher. Those who think that religion is a matter of institutions, hierarchies and formalized practices are happy to rely on positivist methods which can measure such things. On the other hand, for those who believe that religion is defined not by the function it performs in society or by formal content but by the meaning which it has for the individual and its ability to provide some kind of explanation of the purpose of life, what people *think* and *feel* is of vital importance. For these researchers the interpretative approach is the one which will provide the answers. Each method has strengths and weaknesses.

The *strength* of the positivist approach is that it provides concrete data that can be used to support or rebut the claims made by social scientists. For example, the amount of adult church attendance, the number of people who believe in God, the difference in belief between men and women, and the size of the total religious community in the UK. Its *weakness* is that it treats human behaviour without reference to the human concerns of the subject which may give the action a completely different meaning to that understood by the researcher. For example, an individual's failure to attend church might be because of a lack of religious belief but it might be because the individual disagrees with the emphasis of that church (e.g. too male, too 'high' or too 'low') or because she subscribes to a different kind of belief (e.g. some form of New Age belief). At the same time we need to remember that even when positivist methods are used results will be influenced by the interpretation of the researcher. Positivist research is *not* free of human bias and can be influenced by values and beliefs as much as can interpretative research.

The *strength* of the interpretative approach is that it supplies this missing *qualitative* element, i.e. it allows more scope for individuals to put their own interpretation on questions and to give a more personal and diverse response (on the utility of qualitative evidence see *Study Skills Supplement 2: Reading*

Evidence, Section 3). The examples given by the authors are the use of interviews which allow women to express their own views and experiences about religion and in-depth interviews exploring individuals' religious experiences. Other examples (not expanded on in the chapter) are the use of fiction, art and music as a source of evidence and the use of *participant observation* which allows an investigator to participate in and include her or his own experiences of the subject under investigation as a legitimate piece of evidence.

The *weakness* of the interpretative approach is that because it operates in the realm of feelings and opinion the evidence is not subject to the same level of verification as quantitative evidence. It is hard to come up with a reliable way of finding out what people really feel about spiritual matters. Even if we could ask everybody how would we know that their accounts were reliable? They might not be prepared to say anything at all, they might lie and say what they thought we wanted to hear or they might not even know how they felt themselves. This is illustrated by the examination of New Age beliefs and extrasensory experiences with which the chapter concludes. When faced with the question of whether or not there has been an increase in belief in religious knowledge the authors find that statistical evidence is scarce and that it is difficult to define terms and to draw conclusions when faced with the different kinds of interpretative evidence which are available.

Other workbooks have already drummed into you one of the fundamental rules of social science. *Evidence does not speak for itself.* It is one thing to collect evidence about religious belief, or anything else for that matter, but then we have to interpret what it means. This is true of qualitative and of quantitative data. Because of the authority accorded to the scientific method statistics may be seen as being more accurate and reliable – so much so that social scientists often present the results of interpretative studies in a quantitative form. As we have pointed out, however, positivist studies are also influenced by definitions, assumptions, blind spots and other external factors.

Researchers have tried to overcome these problems by combining different kinds of approach; for example, using positivist tools such as surveys and experiments to test subjective accounts of spiritual experiences. However, there is almost always more than one interpretation that can be put on the evidence. The evidence on falling church attendance can be interpreted as 'proving' the secularization thesis. On the other hand, the figures on religious belief suggest that far more people hold religious beliefs than go to church and what people have to say about their own experiences adds yet another dimension. It is for this reason that social scientists tend to prefer to use more than one method and to use evidence not as a means of finally answering a question but as a way of generating new questions.

3 POLITICAL IDEOLOGIES AND THE ENVIRONMENT

Chapters 1 and 2 explored some ideas about what counts as knowledge, the status of different kinds of knowledge and how we find things out. Chapter 3 moves the focus from what we know and how we know it to what we do about what we know. As we noted in the introduction to this workbook, social science knowledge is organized around *theories* about the nature of the social world and *ideologies* which are a set of beliefs and values about how things ought to be and how change can be brought about. There are a variety of different ideologies. For example, Block 3 identified *conservatism, social democracy, liberalism, Marxism* and *feminism* as political ideologies that have influenced the way that we think about social issues and problems, Chapter 2 of this block has shown how religious ideology provides an alternative world-view, and there are, of course, plenty of other ideologies which are not dealt with in this course.

In the same way that theories are tested through the process of the *circuit of knowledge* ideologies are also tested and developed. We choose between different ideologies partly on the basis of how closely they fit with our own vision of the kind of society that we want to see but also on the basis of their accuracy and usefulness in analysing social situations and prescribing ways of dealing with the social world. If the old ideologies are found wanting in this respect it is necessary to develop new ideas that provide better explanations and policies. This is the process that is examined in Chapter 3 in respect of the development of the new ideology of *ecologism* as a response to other ideologies' failure adequately to explain and suggest remedies for the problems of the global environment.

KEY TASKS

Chapter 3, 'Political Ideologies and the Environment'.

- To explore the relationship between knowledge and political action.

- To revisit the concept of political *ideology*.

- To clarify the role of different ideologies in respect of environmental policy.

- To apply the course themes to the comparison between different ideologies.

- To identify the main features of *ecologism*.

- To use the *circuit of knowledge* to evaluate different theories about the environment.

 Now please read Chapter 3, 'Political Ideologies and the Environment', by Simon Bromley and then return to this point in the workbook.

3.1 Knowledge, ideology and the environment

In the same way that Chapter 1 might seem to be 'about' medicine there is a chance that you might fall into the trap of thinking that this chapter is about the environment. So let's dispel that idea straight away and look for the underlying argument relating to knowledge.

3.1.1 Identifying the argument

If you go back to Section 1, you will see that the main theme of the chapter is not the environment as such, but the way that environmental change has challenged our way of thinking and the knowledge that we thought we had about the world. We are not just talking about abstract theories here but about the political ideologies which are responsible for determining how we respond to problems and approach their solution. This is important, not just because it shows us how knowledge evolves, but also because it shows how forms of knowledge and ideology have a direct bearing on practical issues such as the survival of the planet.

If you check Section 1 you will see that it identifies four questions which provide a framework for this chapter. The chapter is concerned with the interaction between political ideology and the environment. It asks:

- What is political ideology and why is it important?
- What are the practical challenges to conventional political ideology posed by environmental degradation?
- How have conventional political ideologies responded to these problems?
- What is the nature of green thinking and how does it differ from conventional political ideologies?

Political ideologies

It is argued that political ideologies are important because they are different ways of understanding (or knowing) the social world and they provide us with a choice of alternative courses of action which will affect the way that society develops and changes. The chapter deals with the three 'mainstream' political ideologies to which you were introduced in Block 3 (and to a lesser extent their Marxist and feminist critiques) and considers their approach to environmental problems. Before we tackle this it would be useful to recap on the main features of each of these in respect of four different aspects – their approach to human nature, politics, economy and social change.

You will find it useful to refer back to your notes on Block 3 here. You may also find your notes on Book 2, Chapter 3 on the market and environmental problems useful.

The grid below shows first the three 'mainstream' ideologies – conservatism, liberalism and social democracy – and then the two main critiques of these, Marxism and feminism.

	Human nature	Politics	Economy	Social change
Conservatism	Imperfect, static; inequalities innate and inevitable.	Emphasis on stability, hierarchy, elite leadership, traditional institutions and 'nationhood'.	Emphasis on rural economy, small firms, traditional industries, low level of state intervention.	Continuity is more important than change. When inevitable, change should be managed by strong leadership.
Liberalism	Self interested.	Emphasis on individual rights and freedoms, minimum state intervention.	Emphasis on competitive markets as the best way of allocating resources and ensuring economic growth; minimum state intervention.	Markets ought to be liberalized so as to allow the 'invisible hand' of the market to bring about equilibrium without state intervention.
Social democracy	A function of social circumstances; improvable by changing conditions.	Emphasis on keeping a balance between interest groups with a democratic state acting as a neutral 'referee' and providing minimum standards.	Emphasis on management of a mixed economy with the state regulating private enterprise and providing welfare and essential services when necessary.	Change ought to be gradual and managed by the democratic state.
Marxism	People can change their nature depending on social circumstances and their own activity.	All societies are divided into classes according to the dominant system of economic production. The dominant class uses the organization of the state to control society in its own interests. Class conflict and changes in the system of production lead to new political systems.	Ownership and control over the means of production determines who benefits from society; the economy should be democratically controlled by the workers, either directly or through the state, and wealth distributed according to need.	Change occurs through class struggle. Full equality can only be brought about by the revolutionary overthrow of the ruling class.
Feminisms	What is called 'human nature' is conditioned by gender relations in society and constructed around gender difference.	The personal is political. Society is patriarchal, most women are excluded from power, social roles are organized to support this; gender inequalities are institutionalized.	The economy is supported by low female wages and the unpaid reproductive labour of women. Women should earn equal pay and be recompensed for their domestic labour or share this with men.	Real social change is not possible without a fundamental change in gender relations, which can only be brought about by collective action.

You will see that each ideology has distinctive features with different implications for policy decisions in a variety of social spheres. These have come about through a process of reaction to and modification of previous ideologies and their application.

Environmental challenges

Although the mainstream political ideologies differ from each other in many ways, it is argued that they share a common tendency which poses particular problems when dealing with environmental problems:

- a belief in a notion of progress which is centred on economic growth
- an approach based on the organization of politics on a national basis
- the placing of human beings in a privileged position at the centre of the universe.

WORKBOOK ACTIVITY 3.1

Re-read Section 2 and make a list of the reasons given for saying that environmental problems pose a challenge to these particular approaches.

COMMENT _____

Ideas about progress which are incorporated in the mainstream ideologies hinge on the belief that this can be brought about by applying the natural sciences and technology to eliminate both natural problems, such as drought, and social ills, such as poverty or famine, thus improving the lot of everybody. But environmental problems are not the result of a simple process of cause and effect involving single factors. They tend to be multi-factoral – that is, they are the product of a complex series of interrelationships which cannot be controlled or predicted. For this reason, attempts to bring about some desired improvement or to solve a particular environmental problem by the application of science are unlikely to succeed and may well have the opposite effect to what is intended.

The problem is made worse by the organization of this idea of progress and development through nation-states which act in their own political and economic interests. In the course of trying to improve the lot of their own citizens nations have inevitably taken a partial view of both the costs and the benefits of any particular action and ignored the total environmental consequences. At the same time it has proved impossible for individual states to overcome environmental problems which are worldwide in their nature.

Finally, it is argued that treating human beings as if they are not part of nature but somehow above it, with superior ethical rights, leads to a fatal blindness about the limits to human capacities. Behaving as if we are lords of all we survey, manipulating nature and even interfering with the genetic structure of life itself might lead to irreversible damage which we are powerless to repair.

Conventional responses

The kinds of solution to these environmental problems which are offered by mainstream political ideologies are divided into two separate camps according to their analysis of the problem and the solution offered. We have mapped these on the grid below.

	Liberalism	Conservatism	Social democracy
Analysis	Environmental problems are caused because market mechanisms do not operate.	Environmental problems arise because market mechanisms are not appropriate for environmental management.	Environmental resources cannot and should not be individually owned, therefore a collective solution must be found.
Solution	Establish ownership rights and prices and then allow the market to operate. If this is not possible use the agency of the state.	Non-intervention in the natural environment.	Democratic decision making. Intervene using the agency of the state.

Green thinking

The radical ecologists' critique of these approaches hinges on their rejection of instrumentalism and anthropocentrism and their adoption of a different worldview and a completely different set of values. In order to assess this critique we must therefore explore those two concepts and get to grips with exactly what they mean and what the implications of the radical stance would be.

WORKBOOK ACTIVITY 3.2

Think about the argument and then jot down your own definitions of the two terms below. Remember, what we are interested in is not just a dictionary definition but a considered explanation of the concepts as they are used here.

Instrumentality

Anthropocentrism

COMMENT

It is clear that when environmentalists refer to instrumentalism and anthropocentrism they are not just using the terms descriptively. Green thinking incorporates a specific view of the ethical relationship between human beings and nature which translates into a political view on the kinds of policy which should be adopted. Instrumentality – the idea of using nature to serve human ends – is frowned on, not because it won't work (that would just be continuing to take an instrumental approach) but because it is seen as ethically wrong. The same is true of anthropocentrism – the belief that the interests of the human species are paramount above all others. Environmentalists oppose policies based on this approach because they put the interests of nature itself above those of just one species.

"THEY USED TO BE THOUGHT OF AS CRACKPOTS."

'Green' alternatives have developed as a critique of existing political ideologies. They argue that conventional theories and explanations are inadequate when it comes to finding solutions to environmental problems and purport to offer an alternative perspective which organizes knowledge in a different way.

WORKBOOK ACTIVITY 3.3

1   What is the difference between *ecology* and *ecologism*?

2   What are the key features of the ecological perspective and how does it differ from the approach of the dominant political ideologies of the twentieth century?

Remember to use your own words or use quotation marks with a page reference.

COMMENT _____

1   The history of the evolution of ecologism shows clearly the incorporation of different kinds of knowledge – including the science of 'relations between organisms and their environment', the study of animal and human behaviour, Greek moral philosophy, and the second law of thermo-dynamics – into the ideology of ecologism that involves a theory about how the world works, social values about how things *ought* to be, and a political programme of action. It is particularly interesting to see how ecologism takes concepts such as energy and efficiency, which are used by physicists and economists, and applies them in a different context.

2   The key features of ecologism and the main differences between this and mainstream political ideologies are mapped on the table which the chapter develops for Activities 3.1–3.5 and 3.7 which is reproduced here as Table 1.

TABLE I   Summary of environmental problems for political ideologies (Table 3.2 from Chapter 3)

	Environmental problems of modern political ideologies	Responses of modern political ideologies	The challenge of green thinking	Green alternatives
Economics	Continued world-wide industrialization is not environmentally sustainable. The market cannot solve environmental problems.	The problem is not one of how *much* growth but what *kind* of growth to pursue. Many environmental problems can be solved by markets if environmental resources are owned and priced properly.	Environmental problems are often unknown and complex. Money is not the measure of everything. What about the future?	Reorganize society away from material growth towards spiritual development. Replace the market with self-sufficiency and direct popular control.
Politics	Environmental problems are typically global in their causes and effects, whereas political authority and control is exercised on a national basis.	International co-operation is possible on the basis of self-interest among states, especially when knowledge about the problem is available and agreed.	If problems are global in scope, then we must move beyond the nation-state and organize politics at a global level as well.	Encourage the development of global citizenship and reconstitute political authority at a global level through extending the UN system.
Culture	Environmental problems are evidence that we cannot subject nature to our control without creating problems.	We are part of nature and therefore we must take an enlightened view of our own interests, which include a healthy environment.	Enlightened self-interest is still *self-interest* (it's human-centred), but what about the interests of the rest of nature?	Respect and protect the interests of the non-human natural world. Need for a new spiritualism. Need for non-reductionist, non-individualistic forms of thinking.

The main claim of green alternatives is that they place nature, not humanity, at the centre of the equation. We need to be careful, however, not to over-simplify by boiling things down too much. It is important to define terms before accepting claims by one side or the other. Since the idea of 'nature' is central to the argument we need to recognize that the term is used in different ways. It is not just descriptive. It is not value free and we need to assess the arguments put forward by ecologists as rigorously as we do those which are put forward by other political ideologists.

3.2 Using the course themes

As we noted above, it can be argued that mainstream ideologies are inadequate to explain and produce solutions for environmental problems for three reasons:

1 They are bounded by the nation-state and traditional power structures.

2 They depend on the idea of scientific certainty.

3 They treat nature and society as separate entities.

The way that we think about these claims can be organized around the three course themes.

3.2.1 Structure and agency

A major obstacle to the solution of environmental problems is one of structure and agency. It is clear that environmental problems are not national in scope, but political power is. The structure of world power depends on the existence of nation-states and, although there are a number of international agencies, it is the sovereign state which is the locus of decision making and the principal agent when it comes to both the initiation of many environmental problems and the implementation of policies to overcome these problems.

Critics of mainstream ideologies argue that their analysis of society fails to take account of the mismatch between the global structure of the problem and the role of national agencies. In assessing this evidence Simon Bromley looks at both sides of the question. Does the fact that mainstream ideologies do not envisage the end of the nation-state mean that they cannot provide any solutions to environmental problems? There are certainly difficulties imposed by international structures but, on the other hand, attaining the only alternative proposed – some supra-national form of power – could be even more difficult than achieving agreement through co-operation or bargaining between sovereign states. Should we work with what we've got or put our energies into changing structures?

'Next one, please!' – 'Progress' versus internationalism

3.2.2 Knowledge and knowing

Green alternatives don't only question the structures for dealing with
environmental problems. They also question our way of knowing about them.
As we pointed out in Chapters 1 and 2, there are a variety of different forms
of knowledge. Simon Bromley examines two criticisms of the role of scientific
knowledge in understanding and prescribing solutions for environmental
problems. Firstly, he assesses the claim by Giddens and Beck that the Western
prioritization of scientific knowledge over other forms of knowledge and
belief is reflected in the ideologies of modernity with their ideas about
'taming' and controlling nature. Secondly, he looks at the claim of many
ecologists that the natural scientific approach is not something neutral but
something which reflects and supports existing, particularly male, systems of
authority.

Look back over Chapters 1 and 2 for any evidence which you might be able to use in discussing these arguments.

C O M M E N T _____

There are a number of examples that you could use. For example, if you turn to Chapter 1 you will find that the discussion of the medical profession provides evidence about the way in which knowledge is socially produced and controlled by the structures of authority. The discussion of the functional role of religion in Chapter 2 highlights the interconnection between knowledge and society and previous chapters in the course also alert you to the role of values even when we are talking about knowledge and science.

_____

What environmentalists are doing when they reject abstract science for spiritual beliefs and more holistic theories is looking for other forms of understanding to support their own social values and world view. If we look at the *evidence* it seems that some of the blanket claims made by environmentalists about the mainstream ideologists' attitude to natural science and technology are not borne out. For example, although 'scientific Marxism' is based on the belief that we can understand and control the environment conservative ideology is extremely sceptical about this and about the idea of 'progress' generally. At the same time not all ecologists reject science as a means of understanding and finding solutions to environmental problems.

3.2.3 Uncertainty and diversity

The course has already introduced you to the idea that society is not simple. Although social scientists attempt to explain, predict and prescribe we are, and always will be, uncertain about many aspects. We live with risk in all aspects of our lives. If we make a personal mistake we must live with the consequences. If a doctor gets things wrong her patients may die. In the context of the nation-state, policies based on faulty social science or political ideology may lead to disaster for millions of people. The same risk applies when natural scientists and social scientists are dealing with environmental problems, only this time it is the future of the planet itself which is at stake.

The kind of interrelationships which exist between different parts of the environment mean that we can never be certain of the results of human intervention. Human beings have always interacted with and modified the environment. The question which the chapter addresses is whether

recent advances in science have made this process qualitatively different
to what has gone before and whether or not it requires a new kind of theory
to understand and analyse it.

WORKBOOK ACTIVITY 3.5

Consider the discussion in Chapter 3, Sections 3 and 4 and identify the different
arguments and evidence which would be used by mainstream ideologists and
environmentalists in answering the following questions:

- Is science now the enemy of progress or the saviour of society?

- Is society at greater risk than ever before?

- Is it possible to find local solutions to environmental problems?

COMMENT

There are no right answers to these questions! To radical ecologists they aren't
even the right questions, because they separate the idea of society from the
rest of the environment. Nevertheless, how we analyse the problem –
whether or not we adopt the mainstream view of our ability to control the
environment or the ecological view of the environment as an integrated
system – will have a significant effect on the policies which are adopted and
on the final outcome. As Section 5 of Chapter 3 points out, the debate
between different ideologies can be seen within the framework of the
circuit of knowledge. The approach of different ideologies is put to the test,
modified and tested again, with new answers and new questions constantly
evolving.

3.3 Ideology and the circuit of knowledge

Chapter 3 uses the framework of the *circuit of knowledge* to test and evaluate
the claims of the rival ideologies (Figure 5).

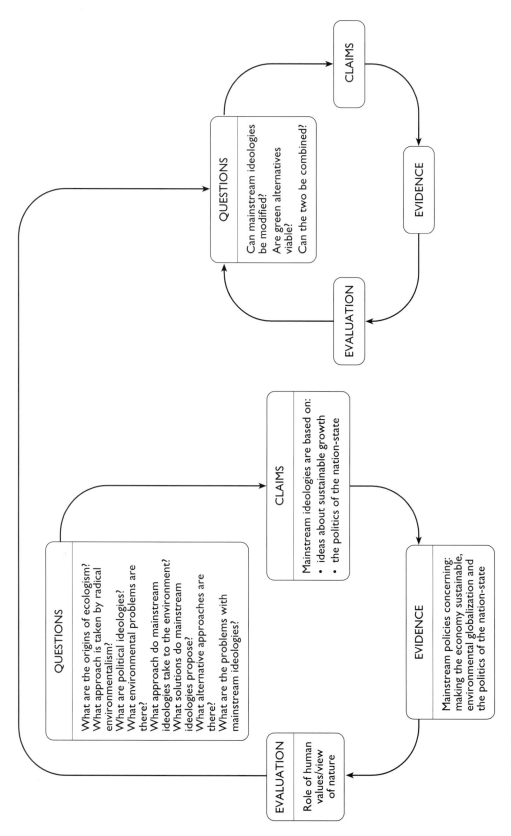

FIGURE 5 Chapter 3 mapped on to the circuit of knowledge

Divided into four steps we can trace the circuit as follows:

- Step 1 defines terms, explores the origins of the ecological perspective and identifies the major features of the argument.

- Step 2 compares the response to environmental problems by mainstream ideologies and radical ecologism.

- Step 3 examines the evidence in relation to specific aspects of the argument (the role of the nation-state and the effect of modern science).

- Step 4 outlines the way in which established ideologies have been modified and an alternative green ideology has been developed.

It is important to note that, as in Chapter 2, there is a mixture of evidence. Some of it is quantitative and refers to measurable aspects of environmental problems, for example. But much of it is qualitative and is directly affected by ideas about ethics and values. In the realms of political ideology these are as important as so-called facts and everything is open to contention – both between the traditional mainstream ideologies and between these and new ideologies such as ecologism.

Environmental change has led to changes in ideology and changes in ideology in turn have an impact on the kind of change which takes place in society. It is this process which is explored in Chapter 4.

4 CHANGING TIMES, CHANGING KNOWLEDGE

Chapter 4 deals with one of the key questions of this block: the role of knowledge, including knowledge in the social sciences, in understanding and influencing social change. This chapter focuses on the apparent explosion of knowledge that can be seen to have characterized contemporary societies by looking at some particular examples of economic and social change and how these have been explained and reflected within the social sciences. Chapter 4 introduces three approaches to change, each of which highlights the importance of knowledge in shaping and influencing transformation over time. They are certainly not the only theories of change, but they are used here to explore examples of the relationship between social and economic change and the knowledge that the social sciences produce to explain those changes.

KEY TASKS

Chapter 4, 'Changing Times, Changing Knowledge'.

- To review the key questions of the block as posed in the first three chapters.

- To understand some of the economic and social background to the 'knowledge revolution'.

- To consider some different approaches to this 'knowledge revolution' within the social sciences.

- To weigh up some of the advantages and disadvantages of the growth of the 'knowledge society'.

 Now please read Chapter 4, 'Changing Times, Changing Knowledge', by Kath Woodward, David Goldblatt and Liz McFall and return to this point in the workbook.

4.1 Chapter 4 and the block so far

Chapter 4 starts with a review of the questions which have been posed in each of the earlier chapters in the book. Before we go on to think about the specific examples of changes that Chapter 4 identifies it would be useful to remind yourself of some of the key issues that have been addressed so far in this block. The block is about knowledge and we started, in Chapter 1, with the question 'what is knowledge?'

WORKBOOK ACTIVITY 4.1

We would like you to make brief notes in response to the questions which framed the first three chapters of Book 5. How does your study of the social sciences so far equip you to answer these questions? The questions are reviewed in Section 1 of Chapter 4.

What is knowledge?

How do we know things?

What do we do about what we know?

COMMENT _____

We noted these points. You might be more specific about the examples you cite, but these are the aspects which we thought summarized our responses.

What is knowledge?

- Knowledge includes practices, ways of thinking, ideas, visual representations and theories and explanations.

- Knowledge is socially constructed, for example through language, cultural practices, and social institutions.

- There are different kinds of knowledge, for example bodies of knowledge covered by subject areas such as medicine and religion.

- There are different categories of knowledge, such as common-sense knowledge, practical knowledge, institutional knowledge, and established and 'expert' knowledge.

- Power is always implicated in the construction of knowledge; some knowledge has higher status than others, some knowledge counts.

- Expert knowledge can be challenged.

How do we know things?

- Social scientists use a range of methods to produce knowledge.

- These methods are designed to produce reliable evidence to support the claims and theories which social scientists develop.

- Knowledge production is linked to the theories and values which underpin the approach.

What do we do about what we know?

- Ideologies form both explanations and theories within the social sciences as well as prescriptions for action.

- An ideology includes some recommendation for action, for example in remedying a problem that has been identified.

- Traditional ideologies may be found to be inadequate in resolving some of the problems that have been created by social and economic change.

- The social sciences have to respond to change to develop not only new explanations of social phenomena but suggestions for how problems can be resolved.

In addressing these questions in the block so far we have been thinking about change. Indeed, our concern with knowledge has been very much with the expansion of different sorts of knowledge and the challenge to traditional expertise, for example in the areas of medical science, religion, and politics and the environment. Chapter 4 picks up on the notion of change and looks particularly at the idea that there has been both an explosion of different forms and sources of knowledge and that there are particular links between social and economic change and this knowledge revolution. The chapter maps out some of the changes which social scientists have highlighted as having particular significance.

4.2 Knowledge and social change

Chapter 4 offers different concepts that can be used to characterize the chronology of changes over the last half of the twentieth century and into the twenty-first charting the movement from Fordism to post-Fordism and into post-modernism in the post-industrial 'consumer' society. There may seem to be a lot of concepts, but they are designed to offer a framework for understanding change. These stages in the development of industrial and post-industrial societies indicate the links between economic and social changes and the ways in which they are classified and understood within the social sciences.

WORKBOOK ACTIVITY 4.2

Look back over Sections 2 and 3. Can you summarize the distinguishing features of each of these concepts used to describe social and economic change? What would you pick out as the key features of each?

COMMENT _____

We made the following brief points:

Fordism: an economic system based on factory mass production, skilled labour and job demarcation, associated with Henry Ford's car production, but applicable to other sectors.

Post-Fordism: used to describe the move from mass production to specialist, flexible production, new technologies and resulting new forms of social organization.

Post-modernism: here seen as developing out of post-Fordism and representing a move away from all-embracing meta theoretical explanations of change and the relationship between the economy and social organization;

arising from the shift in emphasis from production to consumption with a stress on symbolic systems of representation and culture.

4.3 Explaining social change

Chapter 4 picks out three approaches to the growth in the production and dissemination of knowledge in contemporary society:

the knowledge society

the consumer society

the risk society

Each of these approaches involves a different focus, but there are theoretical differences between them as well. In order to clarify your thinking about the different approaches we would like you to look back over the chapter and think about what distinguishes each of them.

"'Be careful'! All you can tell me is 'be careful'?"

The risk society

WORKBOOK ACTIVITY 4.3

How would you define these in your own words? You need to provide a brief definition in just a few sentences.

COMMENT

We have asked you to use your own words so don't worry if you haven't used the same terminology as we have, but this is what we came up with:

KNOWLEDGE SOCIETY

The idea of the knowledge society suggests that many economic changes and changes in production in the late twentieth century featured the development of knowledge, especially I.T. Knowledge has become even more important than raw materials and labour. The production and transmission of knowledge becomes the most important aspect of economic systems and the motor for social and economic change.

CONSUMER SOCIETY

In the latter part of the twentieth century there was an increased interest in consumption and in the activities of consumers. The focus of producers and of social scientists shifted from the production stage in the economic system to looking at consumption as a key stage in providing a framework for understanding change and social relations.

RISK SOCIETY

This approach suggests a model of social change which characterizes western contemporary societies as shifting from low-risk social, economic and political order in which security was related to class position with a minimum safety net provided by the state to one where risk is widespread and unavoidable (regardless of class). Manufacturing industry is in decline and trust in experts has collapsed and the state can no longer provide services and universal social security.

These different approaches have particular emphases, for example the knowledge society focuses on knowledge systems including communications and IT, the consumer society on consumption of goods and services, and the risk society on environmental matters, although each has wide-ranging social and political implications. Each approach develops its own concepts and claims, seeking different evidence to support its theories. Economic change is one aspect which underpins each of these approaches however.

One example of the links between social and economic change and the development of explanation in the social sciences is the move from an emphasis on production to one which focuses more on consumption and is distinguished by the notion of the consumer society. Taking this as an illustration of some of the changes between knowledge and social change how can we summarize some of the ways in which the social sciences relate to such changes?

WORKBOOK ACTIVITY 4.4

How do the social sciences contribute to and explain what Chapter 4 calls the shift from production to consumption?

COMMENT

Our brief notes look like this:

- Daniel Bell's theory of the post-industrial society
  the importance of knowledge
  role of professionals
- Knowledge society technological developments
  new IT developments, speed of communication
- Move from production to consumption
  Fordism → post-Fordism
  concepts of social sciences used to describe and explain economic and social change, from Marxism to post-modernism
  significance of culture, e.g. in post-modern critiques
- Too much knowledge
  risk society, Beck, uncertainty, instability, perceived risks

"A muse! Are you IBM-compatible?"

The knowledge society

4.4 Weighing up the arguments

Each of the three approaches to knowledge and social change considered in Chapter 4 provides a different focus, spotlighting different dimensions of contemporary societies. Thus they are not necessarily conflicting views although they do offer different perspectives on the question of the advantages and disadvantages of the knowledge revolution. For example, the risk society thesis suggests that the explosion of knowledge has produced enormous anxiety and uncertainty rather than the democracy and potential for challenge to traditional sources of knowledge which could be seen as more egalitarian in promoting greater participation and inclusion.

In this section we would like you consider how we could weigh up the three views, not necessarily in relation to each other, but in terms of the strengths and weaknesses of each approach. How might you construct a balance sheet for each view? In order to conduct an evaluation you will need to think about what criteria to use in order to consider what constitutes a strength or a weakness. For example, how well supported is the view? Is there sufficient evidence? How wide ranging is the approach? Can it accommodate a range of different factors? How comprehensive is it? Does it make sense, that is does the conclusion follow on logically from its initial claims?

WORKBOOK ACTIVITY 4.5

Before you start the evaluation it would be useful to note down the key points of each approach starting in the first column of the grid which follows.

	Features	Strengths	Weaknesses
Knowledge society			

	Features	Strengths	Weaknesses
Consumer society			
Risk society			

COMMENT

This is our attempt at filling in the grid.

	Features	Strengths	Weaknesses
Knowledge society	Theoretical Knowledge, marketing Knowledge, and IT and communication processing have become Key economic assets. Therefore transforming economic structures. Groups with Knowledge become more powerful.	Logical claims especially given speed of dissemination of Knowledge. Supported by technological developments, e.g. IT industry and breakdown of traditional heavy manufacturing industry.	Overplays IT and speed of communications systems – medium rather than substance. Narrow focus in some respects downplays economic power therefore not comprehensive.
Consumer society	Patterns of consumption have become more important than production and ownership of means of production in determining social relations and divisions. Culture and symbolic systems contribute to Knowledge about consumption.	Evidence of shift in focus from production to consumption. Primacy of, for example, advertising industry; widespread Knowledge about consumption/consumer goods and services. Some evidence of resistance to commercial promotion.	Underplays power and ownership of means of production and material power in overstating significance of symbolic systems. Therefore not comprehensive.
Risk society	Widespread Knowledge of contemporary risks and their possible consequences is driving force in changing political agenda. Knowledge of risks undermines claims and authority of experts and political leaders.	Logical, coherent claims, evidence of environmental risk and degradation, promotion of anxiety. Some evidence.	Emphasizes particular area of social/economic life, that is environmental risk, therefore not comprehensive. Overstates impending disaster and underplays improvement in life expectancy and life style for most people in West.

The balance sheet of strengths and weaknesses has been informed by the three criteria for evaluating theories that were introduced in *Workbook 4*. Each of the questions posed at the start of the section relates to a criterion of evaluation. For example, the second question we asked – Is there sufficient evidence? – is an important measure of empirical adequacy. The third question – How wide ranging is the approach? – involves consideration of the comprehensiveness of the approach. The final question – Does it make sense? – relates to coherence and involves the internal arguments of the approach, that is how far the conclusion follows on from the earlier stages of the argument. Some of the approaches included here contain different theories, for example the consumer society approach, and the three perspectives are not necessarily in competition, although they do have different emphases and take different stands on the impact of the knowledge revolution. The purpose of this exercise is to develop your critical skills, weighing up different theoretical approaches, illustrating the kinds of questions you need to ask when you are evaluating different theories.

5 REFLECTION AND CONSOLIDATION

As usual you now have the opportunity to consolidate and reflect on your work in this block and complete the TMA question. The Afterword to Book 5 and Side B of Audio-cassette 9 are designed to help you to do this and you should also draw on TV 05.

 Pause now to read the Afterword to Book 5, listen to Side B of Audio-cassette 9 and read the associated notes. Also watch TV 05 around this time (depending on broadcast schedules) and read the associated notes.

Then return to this point in the workbook.

Throughout the course we can trace different strands of the *knowledge and knowing* theme. We have looked at the diversity of different forms of knowledge and how alternative systems have developed to challenge old orthodoxies and bring about social change. In the course it has been argued that in a variety of different spheres of society, including medicine and the natural sciences, management of the environment, the family, the world of work, and relations between states, dominant forms of knowledge which were previously controlled by experts and institutions have been challenged by alternative systems.

The social sciences constitute particular forms of knowledge directed at examining how changes in knowledge come about. This involves analysing the process of how we come to 'know' something, how social scientists gather information and evidence, and how they construct arguments and explanations. As we noted in the introduction to the workbook, synthesis and integration are the final elements in the *circuit of knowledge* whereby aspects of different competing and complementary theories are absorbed, modified and reworked to produce new, and it is hoped more illuminating, ideas and explanations.

In order to complete the circuit we need to go through two separate stages: first we need to bring together (*synthesize*) the different things which have been said about *knowledge and knowing* throughout the block and to sum them up. Then we need to compare and consider the implications of the arguments which have been put forward, and to *integrate* those aspects of each argument to help us develop a new explanation which takes these implications into account and helps us to understand more about the process of studying society and tackling the problems which we identify. In this section we will be concentrating on helping you to synthesize the different aspects of the knowledge and knowing theme.

TABLE 2 Knowledge and knowing in DD100

Course material	Knowledge and knowing: evidence and explanation	Knowledge and knowing: changing knowledges
Introductory Chapter	Section 3: on quantitative and qualitative evidence. Section 5.1: overview.	
Workbook 1	Sections 1–4: on concepts, theories and explanations. Section 6: introduction to the knowledge and knowing theme.	
TV 01		Changing national identities; Britishness.
Study Skills Supplement 1: Reading Visual Images	Using photographs as a source of evidence.	
Workbook 2	Using evidence in the social sciences.	
Book 2, Chapter 2		Contested medical knowledges.
Book 2, Chapter 4		Contested understandings of natural disasters and environmental risks.
TV 02		Changing views of disability.
Study Skills Supplement 2: Reading Evidence	Reading evidence.	
Workbook 3	Sections 1–4: using theories in the social sciences.	
Book 3, Chapters 2–4		Role of political ideologies in social science and their impact on the social world.
Book 3, Chapters 2 and 3	Comparisons of political ideologies on specific topics. Chapter 2: feminism and conservatism on the family. Chapter 3: liberalism and social democracy on the labour market.	
Workbook 4	Section 1.2: globalization – concepts and evidence. Section 2.2: examining the coherence of an argument. Section 2.3: reading quantitative and diagrammatic evidence. Section 3.3: practice with numbers.	Sections 1.2, 1.3, 2.4, 3.2, 4.1 and 5.2.

(continued overleaf)

TABLE 2   *(continued)*

Course material	Knowledge and knowing: evidence and explanation	Knowledge and knowing: changing knowledges
Workbook 4 (continued)	Section 3.4: an evaluation of the inter-nationalist view of globalization. Section 4.2: evaluating the transformationalist argument. Section 5.1: evaluation revisited.	
Book 4, Chapter 1	Section 5: measuring globalization, looking for evidence.	Section 4: the big debates.
Book 4, Chapter 3	Measuring the extent of globalization.	
Workbook 5	Introduction: knowledge and knowing. Section 1.2: scientific and social scientific knowledge. Section 2.3: investigating religion. Section 3.3: ideology and the circuit of knowledge. Section 5: reflection and consolidation.	Introduction: knowledge and knowing. Section 1.1: the social production of knowledge. Section 2.1: the status of religious knowledge. Section 3.1: knowledge, ideology and the environment. Section 4.1: knowledge and social change.
Book 5, Introduction		What is knowledge?
Book 5, Chapter 1	Section 2.1: proof and the construction of scientific debate. Section 3: science and social science ways of thinking.	Section 2: knowledge, medicine and science. Section 4: who are the experts? Section 5: science and society.
Book 5, Chapter 2	Section 2.2: methods and finding out. Sections 3–6: different kinds of evidence about religious belief.	Sections 3–6: secularization and gender, ethnicity and New Age beliefs.
Book 5, Chapter 3	Section 5: evaluating political ideologies.	Section 1: political ideologies. Section 4 the challenge of green thinking.
Book 5, Chapter 4	Section 5: weighing up the arguments.	Sections 1–6: knowledge and social change.
Book 5, Afterword	Social change and the social sciences.	Expert and elite knowledges, knowledge and social change.
TV 05		Changing knowledge about parenting.
Audio-cassette 9		Side B: knowledge and social change.

You can't say we don't help you! You now have a map of the knowledge and knowing theme that you can use to help you to tackle TMA 05 and can refer back to when it comes to TMA 06. But remember, this map is just a one-dimensional version of where you have been. What is most important is that you produce your *own* notes of the theme through the course.

6 ASSESSING BLOCK 5

TMA 05 aims to help you to pull together the material on knowledge and knowing that you have studied in this block and to practice the key skill for the block – the ability to **synthesize and integrate** arguments and evidence.

Before starting on TMA 05 we want you to look at the practice TMA and student notes below (a real TMA used in 2000). Ask yourself the questions that follow and make a plan which identifies the structure of your essay, your main argument and the material from Block 5 which you would use. Then look at our comments and check your plan against the tutors' marking notes at the back of the workbook.

Practice TMA

In approximately 1,500 words, examine the ways in which knowledge can be said to be *socially produced* and how this is related to social change. Illustrate your answer with arguments and evidence from two or more of the chapters in Book 5.

100 marks

Student notes

Note that you are asked to **relate** the idea of the social production of knowledge to that of social change and it is for this that you will earn most credit. Answers making relevant use of the course themes of structure and agency and uncertainty and diversity will also be rewarded. You will probably find it easier to structure your essay if you take a step by step approach to this, *first* examining the arguments about the social production of knowledge and *then* relating these to social change.

In constructing your answer you will find relevant material in all four of the chapters in Book 5. For example:

Chapter 1 introduces the idea that knowledge has an inevitable social aspect and uses the example of the history of the development of medical science to illustrate arguments about subjectivity, objectivity and different ways in which it has been argued that knowledge is socially produced.

Chapter 2 is concerned with how religious knowledge is socially constructed, whether religion has been replaced by scientific knowledge or has simply changed its social basis, how different definitions of religion can influence our conclusions, and how social change has influenced religious belief.

Chapter 3 explains the way that political ideologies are shaped by existing institutions and social interrelationships, how these dictate our response to the environment and how they are influenced by social change.

Chapter 4 explores different ideas about the relationship between knowledge and social change, including economic changes and the shift in emphasis from production to consumption.

Other useful material can be found in Audio-cassette 9, Side B and TV 05 and associated notes.

Planning your essay

Refer back to the essay planning advice in *Workbook 2* and *Workbook 4* and to your tutor's feedback on the essay that you wrote for TMA 04.

Workbook 4 suggests that you ask yourself the following questions before starting to plan the essay:

- What type of question is it?
- What length of answer is required?
- Are there any other specific requirements?
- What is the central subject matter?
- What are the key arguments/conflicting theories on offer?
- Where will I locate my main sources of evidence?
- What will my basic conclusion be?
- How will I structure my answer?

Take a moment to think about your own answers to these questions before consulting my comments below which apply the questions to this practice TMA.

Comments

What type of question is it? The key words in the question are 'examine' and 'illustrate'. 'Examine' entails looking at different aspects and weighing them up. 'Illustrate' means using concrete examples taken from the text as **evidence** to back up the points you are making. You don't have to go through them all in great detail one by one. You need to pick out the key points of each which relate to the question (that is the *synthesis* part of your answer) and then *integrate* those aspects which appear strongest into your own argument and conclusion.

What length of answer is required? We give word limits not because we want you to become obsessed with counting every single word but because we want you to develop the skill of selecting and summarizing appropriate material and expressing an argument concisely. If you go drastically over length, you can expect to be penalized because of your lack of focus and failure to be succinct. But remember that **what** you write is more important than the precise number of words!

Are there any other specific requirements? You have to give examples from two or more chapters. This doesn't mean that you must illustrate every single point in this way but that during the course of the essay you should show your knowledge of the chapters through your use of examples. *Don't forget to provide page references.*

What is the central subject matter? The question is specifically about (i) the social production of knowledge and (ii) the relationship between this and social change. The social production of knowledge is dealt with in every chapter but we don't want lengthy chapter summaries. Pick out those key arguments and examples which relate to the discussion of social change in Chapter 4.

What are the key arguments/conflicting theories on offer? Read the student notes to see if they give you any advice. If they do, don't ignore it! If they don't, go back to your notes or to the chapter summaries and identify and examine those arguments which relate to the question.

Where will I locate my main sources of evidence? Again, read the student notes. Don't forget to use other sources too (TV, audio tapes, etc.) and to refer to the course themes where these are relevant.

What will my basic conclusion be? Your conclusion should follow from your discussion. We want you to bring together the different arguments in the block, to pick out those which you find most relevant and to integrate them into your conclusion.

How will I structure my answer? Make a plan! The simplest way to structure an essay is to say what you are going to do, do it, then say what you have done. When you are building onto this framework you might use some of the chapters as a model (check back on Chapter 3, for example). Remember to:

- **Identify** different ways in which knowledge is socially produced and different arguments about social change.
- **Consider** the different arguments, using examples.
- **Discuss** the interpretation of the evidence and its strengths and weaknesses.
- **Reach a conclusion, stating your reasons.**

This is intended to help you so please give it a go before comparing your plan with the tutor notes at the back of the workbook (pp.72–4). Once you have done that it is on to TMA 05 proper and then on to the final block, Block 6. If you have got this far you've nearly made it. Nothing can stop you now!

 Now turn to the *Assignments Booklet* for TMA 05.

COMMENT ON WORKBOOK ACTIVITY 1.2

You could have used the summaries at the end of each section but we constructed the grid below without them in order to try to use our own words. (It's worth looking at the summaries now, however.)

	Argument	Examples/evidence
Section 2	There is a difference between religious and common-sense knowledge and 'scientific' knowledge; scientific knowledge has come to the fore since the seventeenth century.	The basis of medical knowledge has changed from folk/religious/magical to scientific; the body of medical knowledge and medical training has also changed.
	Expert knowledge develops within a specific community and institutional framework which influences the direction of change and bestows authority on it.	Medical science in the UK developed in the context of the scientific Royal Society and was given authority by the status of the Society and its members; women were excluded.
	The development of institutionalized scientific knowledge privileged objectivity over subjectivity and the rational over the emotional.	Medical science developed using verifiable scientific methodologies; common-sense knowledge and women's knowledge were devalued.
	Scientific methodology aims to produce knowledge that is known to be true because it is subject to objective proof; theories which cannot be scientifically verified are declared to be false; double-blind studies are used to eliminate subjective bias.	Forms of medicine such as homeopathy have been rejected by the medical establishment because they have not been scientifically verified and have not been tested using double-blind methodology.
	Different interest groups have a vested interest in different forms of knowledge.	Medical research is supported by drug companies but this has to pass the scrutiny of 'learned bodies' and scientific journals which impose their own strict criteria.
Section 3	The natural sciences claim to be entirely objective but the way in which science actually works is not so clear cut.	Example of Edmund Stone and the willow bark.

Argument	Examples/evidence
Scientific method is based on proving hypotheses by testing evidence.	
There are a number of different theories about how Knowledge is produced which challenge the idea of scientific objectivity and emphasize social construction.	Doctors use diagnosis to prove that patients are ill. Doctors accept that diagnosis is not an exact science and employ common-sense as well as scientific Knowledge.
Popper: It is only possible to prove a negative not a positive. Scientists should seek to falsify theories not verify them.	
Kuhn: science is interconnected with social change. Scientists develop sets of assumptions, laws and methods (paradigms) which are often replaced by new ones; scientific Knowledge develops in fits and starts according to its social context.	The Royal Society is the product of the scientific revolution which followed the English Civil War.
Foucault: Knowledge is produced through the language and practices used to interpret different phenomena and is therefore related to culture and power; Knowledge and power are inextricably linked.	Illness is 'invented' and classified according to the dominant discourse of the time, medical diagnosis is historically and culturally specific, e.g. in relation to 'humours', 'hysteria', M.E.
Fox Keller: Knowledge is not gender neutral; it is gendered by the social structures through which it is produced.	The (male) medical establishment controls what is 'counted' as illness. Women are a majority in the NHS but not in the higher echelons because they were historically excluded from universities and medical guilds and could not, therefore, practise medicine.

	Argument	Examples/evidence
Section 4	Our definition of knowledge is influenced by the way in which it is represented. There are competing definitions. Whether or not the dominant definition changes depends on the authority of those doing the representing. In the twentieth century the power of the media increased. This may be used by existing sources of authority in support of the existing orthodoxy or it may be used to support new forms of knowledge which challenge that orthodoxy.	SIDS case study.
	Social and cultural assumptions (e.g. about gender) influence theories and privilege expert knowledge over other forms.	Cultural assumptions about motherhood and sources of expertise obscured other explanations for SIDS and the gender hierarchy devalued the evidence of traditional 'female' knowledge.
Section 5	Knowledge is applied and passed on through practices which acquire their own traditions and social institutions.	Traditionally medical practice was embodied in the medical profession, governed by the Hippocratic oath and a system of craft apprenticeship which was limited to men. Today the scientific profession and the academic publishing system perform a similar role in reinforcing existing practices and making dissent difficult.
	Knowledge and power are interrelated. Access to knowledge can be restricted in the interests of particular social groups. Knowledge can be used for political ends.	Case study on smoking and health.

COMMENT ON BLOCK 5 SAMPLE ESSAY QUESTION

Content

The following notes on possible content are based on the guidance given to tutors for marking this question.

The assignment requires students to identify and bring together arguments and evidence about the social production of knowledge from different places in the block and then to relate these to the concept of social change. The key skills here are synthesis and integration. Answers should be in the from of a structured essay, drawing on appropriate theories, evidence and terminology from the sources below and reaching a reasoned and well-supported conclusion.

Key concepts

Knowledge, objectivity, subjectivity, discourse, paradigm, ideology, social construction, social change, risk, uncertainty, post-modernism.

Key sources

Relevant arguments and examples can be used from any of the four chapters. These are summarized below. We do *not* expect students to use them all!

Chapter 1

Section 1 introduces the idea that knowledge takes more than one form. It has an inevitable social aspect because it is communicated and conveyed socially. For example, both common-sense knowledge and medical knowledge have social origins.

Section 2 uses the example of the development of medical science and the roles of the Royal Society and the dissemination of ideas through a social process of academic journals and peer review.

Section 3 outlines the critique of the idea of scientific objectivity by the social constructionist approach.

Section 4 illustrates the influence of the media in representing ideas and the part played by cultural factors in determining which theories are accepted.

Section 5 makes the point that scientists are not passive observers but control knowledge for particular ends. The scientific establishment behaves as a social institution in its own right, shaping the knowledge agents that work within it.

Chapter 2

Section 1 outlines the concern of the chapter with how religious knowledge is socially constructed and whether religion has been replaced by scientific knowledge or has simply changed its social basis.

Section 2 discusses the substantive and functional definitions of religion. It argues that the choice of definition will influence whether you think religion is declining or not and that the interpretative approach allows for different meanings.

Section 3 uses statistics on belief to show that there are differences between different societies and that belief is stronger where more relevant to the social and cultural situation, e.g. in Northern Ireland where there are opposing collective identities or the USA where there have been successive waves of immigrants.

Sections 4 and 5 show how gender and ethnicity influence belief. Religion reflects patriarchal social structures, represents common culture and security and may be a form of identity.

Section 6 argues that new circumstances may lead to a redefinition of religion, e.g. ecologism etc. may be a response to social change such as modernization, globalization and secularization. New Age beliefs may offer new moral meanings.

Chapter 3

Section 1 explains that political ideologies are maps of the social world that aim to tell us how that world works; networks of concepts linked by history and culture formed by abstracting from social life, grounded in social relations and practices. They are linked to social change because they are prescriptive, help to shape understanding and actions, and to alter society.

Section 2 argues that knowledge about the environment is uncertain because science is historically and culturally specific and therefore inadequate to understand complex environmental problems or the environmental implications of economic and other social activity. Knowledge and ideology are territorially bounded – politics makes us view people as separate communities not part of the same world and ideologies fail to recognize natural limits or the natural and social consequences of scientific actions. Nature is no longer separate from society but shaped by it. There is a complex interaction and increasing uncertainty – leading to transition from modern industrial to late modern risk society.

Section 3 describes the response of mainstream ideologies as being shaped by existing institutions and familiar questions, variables and methods; e.g. market economics or managed market, property rights, nation-state, etc.

Section 4 summarizes the ecological perspective, which argues that mainstream perspectives are the products of industrialism and materialism but points out that this is also socially produced. Human beings inevitably interact with the environment and are part of nature and it has been argued that the environmental paradigm is also anthropocentric and rests on ideas about the relationship between man and nature and how this influences society. The definition of nature includes socially generated attitudes and interests, scientific, spiritual or evaluative.

Section 5 relates the discussion to social change. Mainstream ideologies merely adapt their approach to take account of environmental problems. Greens seek to break with previous assumptions but which map is the most use?

Chapter 4

Section 1 argues that changes in knowledge produce social change.

Section 2 outlines the theory of the knowledge society and how this has its origins in Bell's theory of post-industrial society. The knowledge society is distinguished by a concern with how knowledge is produced and used in the economy. It is the main source of innovation, productivity and competitiveness, and social and cultural results will flow from this.

Section 3 traces the origins of the theories of the consumer society, which argue that there has been a significant shift in focus from production to consumption in economic processes which is reflected in and parallels the growth of knowledge about consumption and a move towards greater stress on culture, meanings and representation.

Section 4 outlines the theory of the risk society, which sees the growth in our knowledge of the environment as undermining old forms of social organization and requiring new ones.

Audio-cassette 9

Side B contains relevant discussion.

TV 05

Explores diversity of knowledge and the role of experts in modern parenting.

REFERENCE

Durkheim, E. (1912/1965) *The Elementary Forms of the Religious Life* (trans. J.W. Swain), New York, Free Press.

ACKNOWLEDGEMENTS

Grateful acknowledgement is made to the following sources for permission to reproduce material in this workbook.

Text

Devlin, K. (1999) 'Where Darwin is a dirty word', *Guardian Higher*, 14 September 1999, © Keith Devlin, 1999.

Cartoons

p.13: © Larry. Reproduced with permission of Punch Ltd; p.34: © Raymonde. Reproduced with permission of Punch Ltd; pp.44 and 55: © Sidney Harris; p.47: © Rolf Henn; p.57: © Schwadron. Reproduced with permission of Punch Ltd.

Cover

Image copyright © 1996 PhotoDisc, Inc.

STUDY SKILLS INDEX

IWB = *Introductory Workbook*
WB1 = *Workbook 1*
WB2 = *Workbook 2*
WB3 = *Workbook 3*
WB4 = *Workbook 4*
AC7A = *Notes for Audio-cassette 7, Side A*
WB5 = *Workbook 5*